DATE DUE

T 12943

Evergreen Learning Center

13.25

SNAKES
AND THEIR HOMES

Deborah Chase Gibson

The Rosen Publishing Group's
PowerKids Press™
New York

Published in 1999 by The Rosen Publishing Group, Inc.
29 East 21st Street, New York, NY 10010

First Edition

Book Design: Kim Sonsky

Photo Credits: Cover, title page, pp. 4, 9, 13, 14, 22 © FPG/Gail Shumway; p. 3 © Animals Animals/Marian Bacon; p. 5 © Animals Animals/Doug Wechsler; pp. 6, 18 © Animals Animals/Joe McDonald; p. 7 © Animals Animals/C. W. Schwartz; pp. 10, 17 © Animals Animals/Michael Fogden; p. 12 © Animals Animals/Zig Leszczynski; p. 21 © International Stock/Bob Firth; p. 24 © Animals Animals/Paul Freed.

Gibson, Deborah Chase.
    Snakes and their homes / by Deborah Chase Gibson.
        p. cm. — (Animal habitats)
    Includes index.
    Summary: Presents an overview of different kinds of snakes and how and where they make their homes.
    ISBN 0-8239-5310-6
    1. Snakes—Juvenile literature. 2. Snakes—Habitat—Juvenile literature. [1. Snakes.]
    I. Title. II. Series: Gibson, Deborah Chase. Animal habitats.
QL666.06G47 1998
597.96—dc21   98-15388
                                                                  CIP
                                                                   AC

Manufactured in the United States of America

CONTENTS

1 Snakes of the World   4
2 What Are Snakes Like?   6
3 Deserts   8
4 The Horned Viper   11
5 Tropical Rain Forests   12
6 The Tree Boa   15
7 Burrowing Snakes   16
8 Snakes in the Water   19
9 Sea Snakes   20
10 Snakes and Humans   22
   Web Sites   22
   Glossary   23
   Index   24

SNAKES OF THE WORLD

Deserts, **rain forests** (RAYN FOR-ests), rivers, grasslands, and even the sea are all **habitats** (HA-bih-tats) of snakes. Snakes are **reptiles** (REP-tylz). Reptiles are cold-blooded. They need heat from the sun or a warm rock to warm their bodies. Because of this, very few snakes make their homes in the colder parts of the world.

Snakes, such as this green tree python, have long backbones and many ribs.

Close to 2,700 **species** (SPEE-sheez) of snakes roam the earth. Some snakes are as thin and short as a pencil. But others, like the **reticulated python** (reh-TIH-kyoo-lay-ted PY-thon) of southeast Asia, can grow as long as a school bus!

▼ The garter snake is very common and harmless to humans.

WHAT ARE SNAKES LIKE?

Snakes have long bodies. Their skin is made up of thousands of individual **scales** (SKAYLZ). Snakes don't have legs. They move by sliding on their bellies. Most snakes live on the ground. Some live in trees or water. Snakes don't have ears or eyelids. They "hear" by feeling **vibrations** (vy-BRAY-shunz) in the ground. Snakes stick out their long, forked tongues to "taste" the air for food. Some snakes kill their **prey** (PRAY) with **poison** (POY-zun) that comes out of their sharp fangs.

◀ The northern copperhead uses its tongue to smell prey.

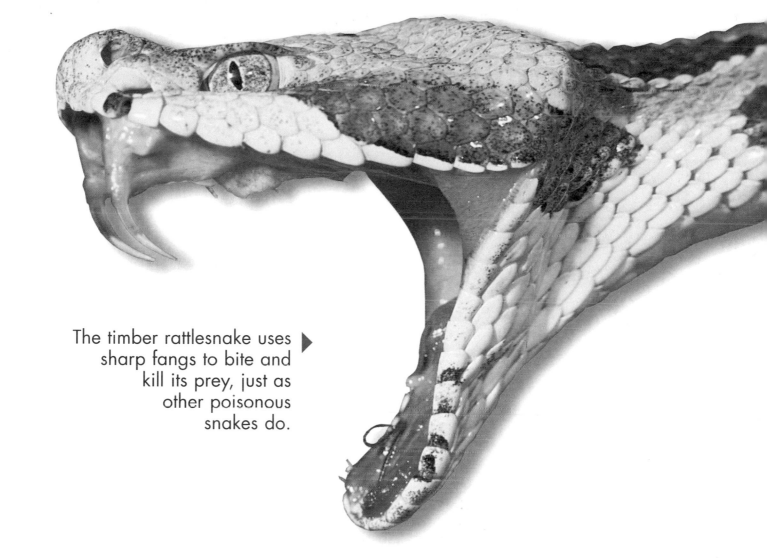

The timber rattlesnake uses sharp fangs to bite and kill its prey, just as other poisonous snakes do. ▶

Others wind their bodies around the prey and squeeze it to death. Snakes can't chew their food, so many swallow their prey whole, often while it's still alive.

DESERTS

Many kinds of snakes **thrive** (THRYV) in deserts. Deserts are dry and hot. **Temperatures** (TEM-pruh-cherz) in deserts can be as high as 100°F or 38°C. It may not rain there for years at a time. Deserts cover much of Africa, Asia, Australia, the Middle East, and the southwestern United States.

When humans get hot, we lose **moisture** (MOYS-cher) through our skin by sweating. The scaly skin of a snake keeps moisture inside its body. This makes it possible for snakes to live in the dry heat of deserts. The heat of the desert actually helps cold-blooded snakes keep up their body temperature.

Rattlesnakes, like the diamondback rattler, are the most dangerous snakes in America. Rattlesnakes will usually ▶ bite people only if someone steps on them.

THE HORNED VIPER

The horned viper lives in the deserts of the Middle East and North Africa. A horned viper is the color of sand and can grow to be almost three feet long. Each has two small horns sticking up out of its head, one over each eye. These horns give the horned viper its unique look and name. Its prey includes mice and lizards.

Even though horned vipers need the heat of the desert, at certain times during the day, they can get too hot. Horned vipers will then **burrow** (BUR-oh) into the sand. Burrowing and the sandy color of their skin help horned vipers hide from **predators** (PREH-duh-terz).

◀ Like all snakes, the horned viper sheds its skin several times each year.

TROPICAL RAIN FORESTS

Many snakes live in the habitat of **tropical** (TRAH-pih-kul) rain forests of Africa, Asia, Australia, and South America. Tropical rain forests have high temperatures and lots of rain.

These warm, green forests are home to more than half of all the species of plants and animals in the world. Beautiful birds, such as toucans, animals like lemurs, opossums, and sloths, and thousands of kinds of insects are just some of the creatures that are found in rain forests.

Snakes, such as this Macgregor's viper, can bend in almost ▶ all directions.

This young emerald tree boa, like other tree boas, uses its strong tail to hold on to tree branches.

THE TREE BOA

The rain forests of South America are the habitats of tree boas. They make their homes in trees. In fact, tree boas don't leave their trees very often. They usually come down only to go for a swim in a river or to slither around on the ground for a little while.

The tree boa hunts by hanging from a branch and swinging its head from side to side. If it feels heat on both sides of its head, a tree boa knows a meal is nearby.

Tree boas don't always wrap themselves around branches. Sometimes they drape their bodies over a branch instead. This leaves a tree boa ready to catch a fast-moving meal if one comes close enough.

BURROWING SNAKES

Did you know that snake habitats include places like underground tunnels? Minute snakes are burrowing snakes. These little snakes can be from six inches to over three feet long with bodies made especially for digging. Minute snakes look a lot like worms. Their heads are the same size and shape as their tails.

Burrowing snakes dig tunnels to live in. To make a tunnel, a burrowing snake **bores** (BORZ) its head into the sand or ground. It uses its tail for support. These snakes will also take over tunnels made by insects, such as termites. Minute snakes spend so much time underground that most don't see very well. Some are even blind.

This giant blind snake is just one of many different species of blind snakes. Just like minute snakes, some blind snakes are burrowers. ▶

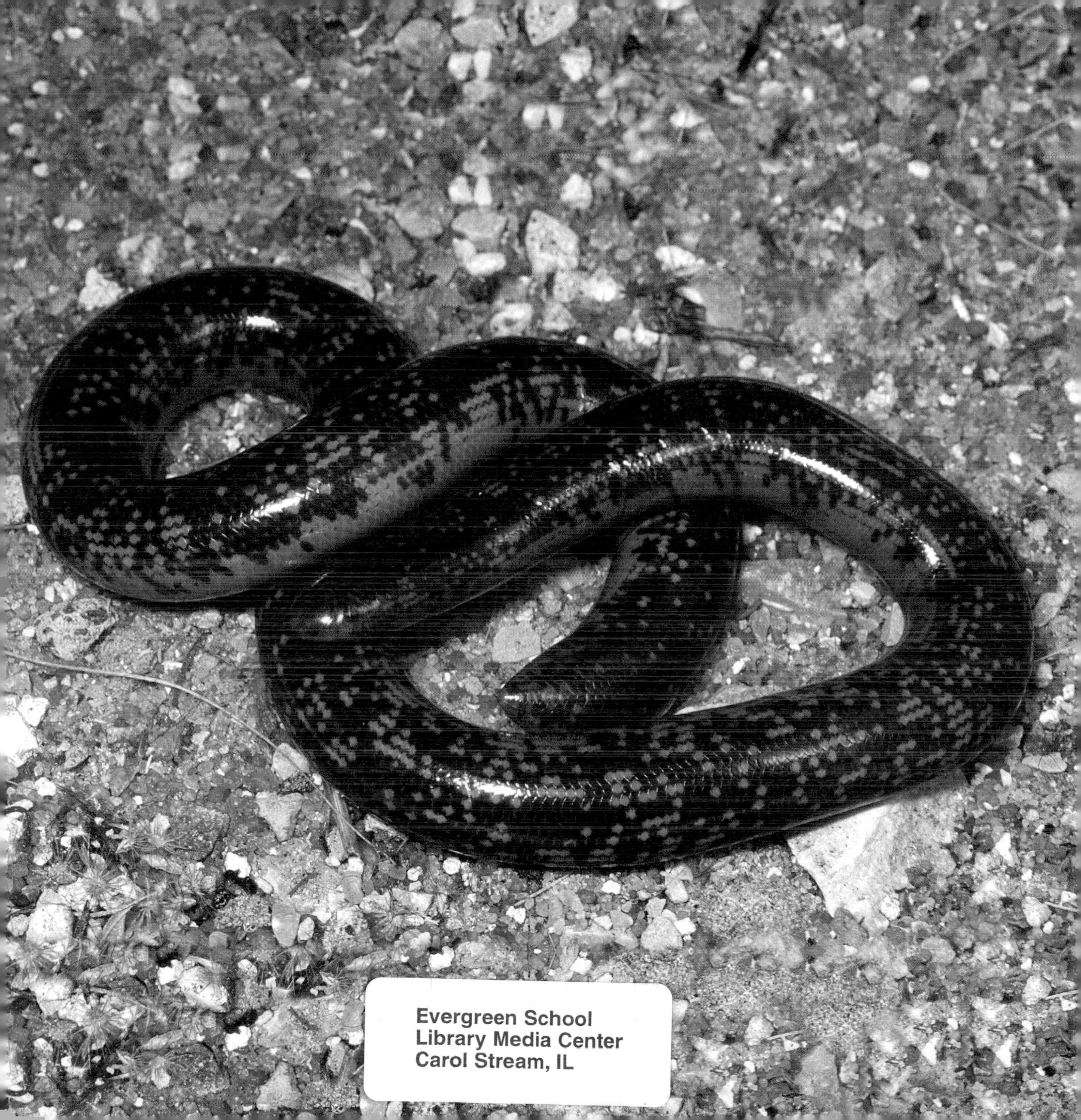

SNAKES IN THE WATER

Most snakes are good swimmers. In fact, wet, swampy places are the habitats of certain types of snakes. The North American water moccasin makes his home in freshwater lakes and rivers. This dark brown snake usually grows to be about three feet long, but can grow as long as six feet.

When they're not slithering about in the water, water moccasins like to sun themselves on warm rocks. They are good climbers and often relax on tree branches that hang over the water.

This poisonous snake is also known as a cottonmouth snake. Water moccasins eat fish, frogs, and other animals they find in their habitat.

◀ When a water moccasin is startled, it holds its head up and shows the inside of its mouth—which is white, like cotton. This is why the water moccasin is also called a cottonmouth.

19

SEA SNAKES

Some snakes live in the ocean. About 35 species of sea snakes live along the coastlines of the tropical Pacific and Indian Oceans. Northern Australia has a few sea snakes as well.

Sea snakes have flat bodies and tails that look like oars that help them swim. Most sea snakes stay in the water. Many don't have the kind of skin that allows them to move on land. But some sea snakes are able to leave the water to lay eggs on coral reefs. These sea snakes have skin like that of land snakes.

Sea snakes eat small fish. The sea snake is the prey of seabirds, sharks, and large fish.

Sea snakes can stay underwater for up to eight hours at a time. ▶

SNAKES AND HUMANS

Humans are the biggest threat to snakes and their habitats. The **destruction** (dih-STRUK-shun) of rain forests and the pollution of the air and ocean all harm the habitats of snakes and other animals. Snakes and all living creatures need clean, safe habitats in which to live. Scientists are hard at work trying to find ways to protect animals and their habitats. By learning more about snakes and other animals, people can show that they care for and respect nature and its creatures.

WEB SITES:

You can learn more about owls on the Internet. Check out this Web site:

http://www.shadeslanding.com/jas

GLOSSARY

bore (BOR) To make a hole in the ground by digging or pushing.

burrow (BUR-oh) To dig a hole in the ground for shelter.

destruction (dih-STRUK-shun) Terrible damage.

habitat (HA-bih-tat) The surroundings where an animal lives.

moisture (MOYS-cher) Water or other liquid.

poison (POY-zun) Something that can make you very sick or kill you.

predator (PREH-duh-ter) An animal that kills other animals for food.

prey (PRAY) An animal that is eaten by other animals as food.

rain forest (RAYN FOR-est) A very wet area that has many kinds of plants, trees, and animals.

reptile (REP-tyl) The group of cold-blooded animals that includes crocodiles, lizards, snakes, and turtles.

reticulated python (reh-TIH-kyoo-lay-ted PY-thon) The largest snake in the world.

scales (SKAYLZ) The thin, flat pieces of skin that form the outer covering of snakes.

species (SPEE-sheez) A group of animals that are very much alike.

temperature (TEM-pruh-cher) How hot or cold something is.

thrive (THRYV) When an animal or plant does well living in certain conditions.

tropical (TRAH-pih-kul) An area that is very hot and humid.

vibration (vy-BRAY-shun) A rapid movement that can be felt through the ground.

INDEX

B
bore, 16
burrow, 11, 16

D
destruction, 22

H
habitat, 4, 12, 15, 19, 22

M
moisture, 8

P
poison, 6
predator, 11

prey, 6, 7, 11

R
rain forest, 4, 12, 22
reptile, 4
reticulated python, 5

S
scales, 6
scaly, 8
species, 5, 12, 20

T
temperature, 8, 12
thrive, 8
tropical, 12

V
vibration, 6